TIMES PAST

GREAT CITIES

Manchester

TOP LEFT: A MANCHESTER MILLWORKER, *c* 1935; CENTRE: TRIUMPHAL ARCH, TRAFFORD PARK, *c* 1910;
TOP RIGHT: CHILDREN IN THE MOUTH OF A REPLICA WHALE, BELLE VUE, 1955;
MAIN PICTURE: ST ANN'S SQUARE, 1905

ROBERT GIBB

MYRIAD

LONDON

THE CITY CENTRE

Mancunium, a Roman fort, was sited at the crossroads of some of the most strategic routes in Roman Britain. From this historic beginning the modern city of Manchester developed. The Industrial Revolution fuelled a tremendous growth in population and the city's fine Victorian architecture reflects its wealth and importance since that time

ABOVE: **MARKET STREET, 1895.** Horse-drawn trams ferry passengers to and from the busy city centre. Destinations include Alexandra Park, Brooks' Bar and Hyde Road. The pavements are heaving with shoppers and business people. Market Street was widened between 1822 and 1834 at a cost of £200,000.

ABOVE: **PICCADILLY, c 1910.** The final stages of the demolition of the Royal Infirmary that was built on this site in 1775. Part of the building, which is still intact, is the accident room on Parker Street. The tower in the background is part of the Minshull Street law courts.

BELOW: **PICCADILLY GARDENS, 1936.** A view of the gardens from Portland Street looking towards Lewis's department store on the other side. The gardens were once a claypit until Lord Mosley donated the land for use as a public garden in the late 18th century.

ABOVE: **PICCADILLY, c 1890.** The Royal Infirmary on the right-hand side casts a dark shadow over Piccadilly. On the corner of Mosley Street stands the statue of Robert Peel, erected in 1856, which looks towards Oldham Street. This was Manchester's first outdoor statue financed by public subscription. Over £3,000 was collected within a week.

ABOVE: **EXCHANGE STATION AND CROMWELL'S STATUE, *c* 1885.** The imposing statue of Cromwell looks up Victoria Street. Erected in 1875, in 1968 it was moved to Wythenshawe Hall which, during the Civil War, the Roundhead troops used as a billet. Exchange Station was demolished in the mid 1980s and replaced by a car park.

BELOW: **MARKET STREET, 1953.** Crowds of shoppers throng the city centre dodging traffic on the corner of Cross Street, looking up towards Piccadilly in the distance. The Arndale Centre now occupies the left-hand side of Market Street from Burton's the tailors to Debenhams in the distance. When the Arndale was completed in 1979 it was the largest covered retail area in Europe.

ABOVE: **MANCHESTER CATHEDRAL, 1936.** The memorial service for the death of King George V (1910-1936) in Manchester Cathedral. The king had been a regular visitor to Manchester, particularly during the First World War and its aftermath. In 1934 he opened the new Central Library.

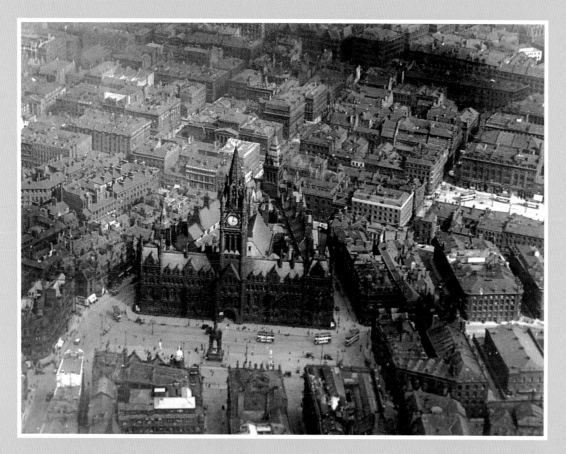

LEFT: **ALBERT SQUARE**, *c* 1922. An aerial view of the town hall and surrounding buildings. Albert Square and St Peter's Square are clearly visible.

BELOW LEFT: **ALBERT SQUARE**, *c* 1950. Manchester Town Hall dominates Albert Square. The skyline from the square has changed very little to this day.

BOTTOM LEFT: **THE ART GALLERY AND MOSLEY STREET, 1880.** A police officer stands at the junction of Princess Street and Mosley Street waiting to direct traffic. In the foreground is the Manchester Art Gallery. The building was designed by Charles Barry and opened in 1834; it has operated as the City Art Gallery since 1882.

BELOW: **SPRING GARDENS**, *c* 1910. A busy scene on the cobbled Spring Gardens outside the Post Office. In the background is the new Midland Bank in its final stages of completion. This huge Art Deco-style building is clad in white stone and was designed by Sir Edwin Luytens who also designed the cenotaph in St Peter's Square.

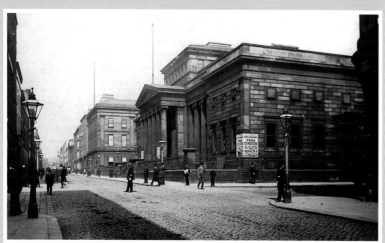

ABOVE: **SPRING GARDENS POST OFFICE, *c* 1898.** The central Post Office in Manchester employed hundreds of staff to deal with mail and telegraph post. Smart appearance was essential and all staff were required to dress in collar and tie.

ABOVE: **THE MANCHESTER GUARDIAN BUILDING, *c* 1905.** The original *Manchester Guardian* and *Manchester Evening News* building stood opposite the Exchange building on Cross Street. The papers were printed in the basement and then rushed over to horse-drawn carts for distribution. The ground floor contained the advertising department. In 1970 the papers moved from Cross Street to new offices in Deansgate. They had been written and printed at the Cross Street building since 1886.

LEFT: **MARKET STREET AND ITS JUNCTION WITH CROSS STREET, 1914.** Since the 13th century Market Street has been at the centre of the city's retail trade. The first horse-drawn omnibus service in Britain was started in 1824 between Pendleton and Market Street.

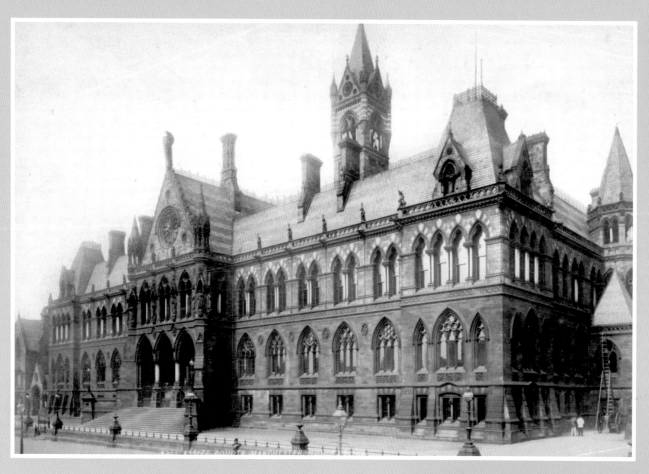

LEFT: **THE ASSIZE COURTS,** *c* 1895. Begun in 1859 the Assize Courts were the first major work of Alfred Waterhouse (1830-1905) who also designed Manchester Town Hall and whose Gothic-style architecture is so important in the Manchester streetscape. Located close to Strangeways Prison, the courts were constructed at a cost of over £13,000. The statue of Moses, known as the lawgiver, stood over the entrance. The courts were badly damaged during the Blitz of 1940-41 and were subsequently demolished.

ABOVE: **MANCHESTER CENTRAL LIBRARY UNDER CONSTRUCTION, 1932.** Manchester was the first local authority to set up a public lending and reference library and the first library was opened in 1852 at the Hall of Science, Campfield (on the site of the current Air and Space Museum). The collection soon outgrew these premises and the architect E Vincent Harris (1876-1971) won an architectural competition to build the new Central Library and Town Hall extension. In 1930 the Prime Minister, Ramsay MacDonald, laid the foundation stone and in 1934 the new library was opened by King George V. At the time it was the largest public library in the country and it is still one of the busiest.

ABOVE: **CHETHAM'S SCHOOL, 1938.** Young boys in the dining hall of the famous school with its superb inglenook fireplace. This ancient manor house, which dates from 1421, is the most complete set of medieval buildings to survive in north-west England. It occupies the site of the manor house of Manchester which, together with the parish church (now the Cathedral), formed the core of the medieval town. It was saved from destruction in 1651 by Manchester cloth merchant Humphrey Chetham whose bequest allowed for renovation of the building and the establishment of a school to educate 40 poor children. In 1969 Chethams became a co-educational school for young musicians.

ABOVE: **DEANSGATE, 1900.** Deansgate was the home of many quality shops, businesses and services. The Old Picture Shop displayed its paintings outside to catch the eye of potential customers.

BELOW: An aerial view of the **DEANSGATE** district which clearly shows the City Exhibition Hall, St Matthew's and St John's churches, the Opera House, Sunlight House and, on the right, the LNER goods yard.

ABOVE: **KING STREET** *c* 1900. Most of the property on King Street consisted of business or professional accommodation. Houses had been steadily demolished during the preceding years to make way for prestigious office buildings and banks. In the distance the Manchester Reform Club displays traces of its Gothic architecture. Built between 1870-1 by Edward Salomons, it was one of the largest purpose-built clubhouses outside London. A grand staircase runs the height of the building from the spacious entrance hall, and on the ground floor there are magnificent lavatories with marble washbasins.

TRANSPORT

Manchester can lay claim to a clutch of British transport "firsts" — the first passenger railway line was the one from Manchester to Liverpool, served by the first passenger railway station at Liverpool Road. Barton Airport was the UK's first municipal airport and the Manchester Ship Canal was the first canal to link ocean-going ships to a British city

THE MANCHESTER SHIP CANAL stretches 36 miles from the southern shore of the Mersey estuary to within a mile of Manchester city centre. Opened in 1894, the canal was built to avoid the high cost of shipping goods through Liverpool Docks.
ABOVE: TRAFFORD ROAD BRIDGE, 1894. The Swing Bridge was one of seven bridges to span the canal. Built in 1892 by Butler and Co of Leeds, it was the smallest bridge on the canal but, at 1,800 tons, the heaviest. Just beyond the bridge is Pomona Dock.
RIGHT: MANCHESTER SHIP CANAL, *c* 1890. Salford dock number 7, on a misty day as a ship sets sail with a cargo bound for Liverpool.

ABOVE: MANCHESTER SHIP CANAL, DRY DOCK, 1901. The *Elswick Lodge* in dry dock having her hull repaired and painted. The two dry docks at Trafford Park were large enough to repair ships of all sizes including ocean-going liners.

ABOVE: **HORSE-DRAWN OMNIBUS, 1880.**
Operating on the route from Cheadle to
Manchester via Didsbury, this privately-owned
carriage could carry up to 42 passengers bound
for the city centre. Twelve people had to brave the
elements by sitting on the open upper deck.

INSET: **TICKET COLLECTOR, 1917.** In the early
part of the 20th century the Lancashire and
Yorkshire Railway was one of the most heavily
worked railway networks in the country and
employed a small army of uniformed inspectors
to check tickets.

BELOW: **MARKET STREET, 1930.** A line
of passengers join the number 35 tram.

BOTTOM: **PICCADILLY BUS STATION, 1935.**
Passengers wait patiently in the rain for the bus home.

ABOVE: **DEANSGATE, 1901.** A crowd of trackmen gather around the newly-laid St Mary's Gate
junction on Deansgate — a vital part of the city's first electric-powered tramway from Albert
Square to Cheetham Hill.

BELOW: **ALBERT SQUARE, 1901.** The official opening of the electric tramway on June 6 1901 was
attended by thousands of spectators and officials, the crowds controlled by numerous police
officers. Over 500 new trams were used between 1901 and 1903. The Queen's Road depot
accommodated over half the vehicles and Hyde Road depot was built to house the balance.

ABOVE: **GAS GUZZLER, 1939.** This *Manchester Evening News* photograph from early on in the war is of the first car to be converted to run on gas. Nearly two decades on, Manchester citizens (above left) are still protesting about fuel rationing!

LEFT: **MINSHULL STREET, 1905.** The canal bridge next to the law courts undergoing repairs.

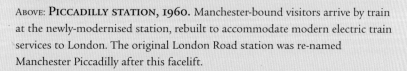

ABOVE: **PICCADILLY STATION, 1960.** Manchester-bound visitors arrive by train at the newly-modernised station, rebuilt to accommodate modern electric train services to London. The original London Road station was re-named Manchester Piccadilly after this facelift.

RIGHT: **STEAM TRAIN, STALYBRIDGE, 1966.** Steam trains like this one which operated on the trans-Pennine route to Leeds were largely phased out in the 1960s to make way for diesel and electric-powered stock.

ABOVE: **MANCHESTER AIRPORT, JULY 1930.** Airport dignitaries await the arrival of Lady Bailey, one of the pioneering figures in women's aviation, for the King's Cup air race around England. Established by King George V as an incentive for the development of British light aircraft and engine design, the event was watched by over 30,000 people.

ABOVE: **CHAT MOSS AERODROME, 1931.** Film actress Frances Day poses with a De Havilland DH 60 X Moth with the emblem of Manchester Airport painted on the fuselage.

RIGHT: **MANCHESTER AIRPORT, c 1950.** In the golden age of air travel there were very few passengers. Compared with today, when more than 150,000 passengers a year pass through the departure lounge, this photograph of the main reception area at Ringway shows how few people travelled by air at this time.

ABOVE: **MANCHESTER AIRPORT, 1932.** The City Council wanted to be the first in Britain to have a licensed airfield, and Barton was chosen to replace an earlier airfield at Alexandra Park when the landowner refused to sell the site. Barton opened in 1930 and included a control tower and large hangar. With only a grass runway it soon became unsuitable for larger aircraft and an area south of Manchester was earmarked for development. Named Ringway, it took three years to construct and opened in June 1938.

HEAVY INDUSTRY

Manchester has long been at the heart of Britain's transport manufacturing industry – particularly the building of aircraft and locomotives. The establishment of these highly skilled enterprises brought in its wake a network of support industries to the area

ABOVE: **AN AERIAL VIEW OF MOSTON, 1935.** The electronics giant Ferranti moved to the north-west from London tempted by lower land costs and wages. Pioneering work on the development of computers — including the first basic computer known as "the baby" — was done at Moston in collaboration with the University of Manchester; the Ferranti archive was based there until 1990.

ABOVE: **HULME, 1907.** The first car built by Rolls Royce in 1904 parked in Cooke Street, Hulme. This car sold for £395 when it was built — today it is valued at approximately £250k. The famous radiator badge, known as the "Spirit of Ecstasy", was introduced in 1911 and was based on Eleanor Thornton, the secretary and mistress of Lord Montague of Beaulieu, a Rolls Royce customer.

ABOVE: **CROSSLEY ELECTRIC BATTERY VEHICLE, 1935.** Francis and William Crossley formed their famous company in 1867. Development work on these electric-powered vehicles stopped before the Second World War, when the firm shifted production to the manufacture of military vehicles.
LEFT: **OLD TRAFFORD,** *c* 1920. A car is re-fuelled on the forecourt of H&J Quick, an authorised Ford dealer.

RIGHT: **MANCHESTER SHIP CANAL, 1929.** Locomotives from the Beyer Peacock Railway Works (known locally as Gorton Tank) waiting to be loaded onto ships for delivery around the world and (below) being craned into position. The works at Gorton Foundry on Railway Street began production in 1854 and manufactured more than 8,000 locomotives. The works closed in 1966; today the buildings are used as a depot for Manchester Corporation, although some of the railway lines can still be seen.

BOTTOM: **THE CROSSLEY WORKS IN OPENSHAW, 1934.** This important workshop employed many skilled craftsmen from coach builders to coach painters. Here we see skilled men painting motor bus bodies before they are fitted to the chassis.

ABOVE: **CLOVER MILL, ROCHDALE, 1952.** The great fire at the mill on June 5 1952 caused over £1m worth of damage. More than 250 firemen battled for nine hours to extinguish the blaze, thought to have started when a blow lamp exploded in the basement.

THE COTTON CONNECTION

Manchester's wealth was founded on cotton. Many of the grandees of the industry had radicalism in their bones — not only did they fight to repeal the hated Corn Laws but, in the wake of the Peterloo Massacre of 1821, they set up their own newspaper — the Manchester Guardian. Other newspapers followed and soon virtually every national newspaper had an office in the city

BELOW: **THE OFFICES OF THE DAILY HERALD, OXFORD STREET**, *c* 1930. Sub-editors prepare copy before the paper goes to press. Launched in 1911, the *Daily Herald* moved to its Oxford Street premises in 1930. This radical title was set up in the aftermath of a printworkers strike and became the voice of the labour movement – although it was highly critical of the Labour government of Ramsay MacDonald. It was the first newspaper to sell 2m copies a day and the only paper to fully support the suffragettes in their fight for the vote.

ABOVE: **ANCOATS**, *c* 1939. Reels of paper arrive on wagons at the *Daily Express* building in Ancoats. This impressive glass structure was designed by Sir Owen Williams and built in 1939. It is one of the first examples of the Modernist style in Manchester. The triple height rooms on the ground floor were built to accommodate the printing presses.

LEFT AND RIGHT: **THE CROSS STREET OFFICES OF THE MANCHESTER GUARDIAN AND MANCHESTER EVENING NEWS.** The papers and their printworks were based at Cross Street from 1886 until the move, in 1970, to Deansgate, where many important editorial and advertising departments are currently located. The photograph (right) shows a crane outside the Cross Street building as the papers prepare to move in August 1970; the offices were finally demolished in 1972.

A **Manchester cotton mill**, *c* 1935. Cotton manufacture developed in Lancashire due to an extensive labour force and a plentiful supply of soft water. In the 1830s approximately 85% of all cotton manufactured worldwide was produced in Lancashire.

LEFT AND ABOVE: **WOMEN TEXTILE WORKERS.** Working alongside men in the mills and earning a wage meant that Lancashire women became known for their independence and self-reliance, and many campaigned for radical causes — from votes for women to equal pay. The woman pictured here is working as a "beamer" or checker. Notice how carefully she is examining the fabric for any faults.

ABOVE: **FABRIC PRODUCTION** involved turning raw cotton, which was usually imported from the USA via Liverpool, into finished cloth. Many of the hot and dirty activities were performed by women, who were overseen by male machine operators. The aristocrats of the cotton industry were the men known as "mule-spinners" – they earned a "family wage" and their wives did not have to go out to work.

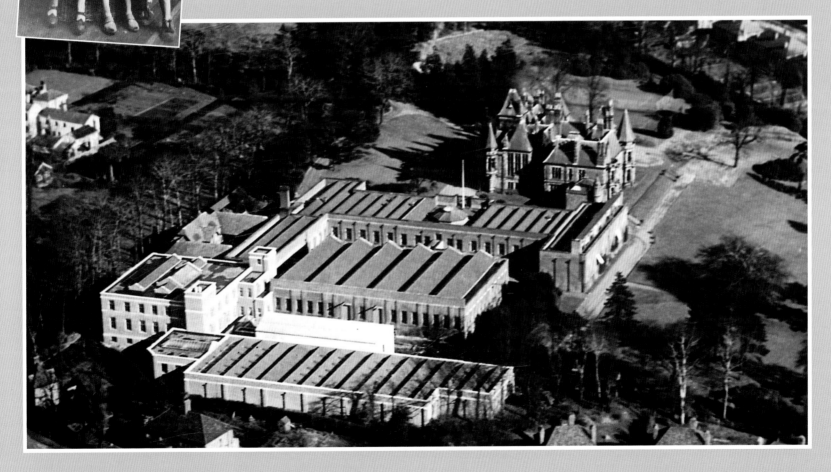

ABOVE: **THE SHIRLEY INSTITUTE, DIDSBURY, 1936**. The Victorian house north of the laboratories was described by Sir Nikolaus Pevsner as "the grandest of all Manchester mansions". Named The Towers it was originally owned by John Edward Taylor, the proprietor of the *Manchester Guardian*. In 1874 it was bought by the engineer Daniel Adamson and in 1882 a meeting was held there at which the decision to set up the Manchester Ship Canal was taken. In 1920 The Towers was purchased by the British Cotton Industry Research Association, and named the Shirley Institute after the daughter of a Stockport MP, William Greenwood. The first purpose-built laboratories at the institute were opened in 1922 by the Duke of York.

LEISURE — WHIT WALKS AND BELLE VUE

In its heyday, Belle Vue — "the showground of the world" — was the greatest outdoor attraction in the United Kingdom. As late as the 1960s it was the country's largest inland amusement park and the most important provincial zoo

ABOVE: **AN AERIAL PHOTOGRAPH OF THE GIANT BELLE VUE SITE, 1922.** In the foreground the caterpillar and "bobs" and in the distance the boating lake in the centre of which was the famous Jennison clock tower. It was named after John Jennison who started the park in 1836 and was demolished in 1949. A windmill was erected in its place. In 1963 the lake was drained and filled in after the water supply from the Stockport branch canal came to an end.

RIGHT: **BELLE VUE KEEPER, 1920.** The monkey terrace was added to the side of the elephant house in the late 1890s and was an extremely popular attraction for children, especially at tea-party time.

FAR LEFT: **BELLE VUE,** *c* **1900.** Among the many attractions the figure of eight and the toboggan rides dominate the skyline. As newer rides eventually became more popular and maintenance costs rose, so the "bobs" were demolished. LEFT: **BELLE VUE, 1946.** Visitor numbers exceeded all expectations, even in the aftermath of the war. In the crowd servicemen can be seen, enjoying a day out while home on leave. The caterpillar was the most popular ride of the park and at peak times an hour's wait was quite common.

ABOVE: **CAESAR'S PALACE** has had many uses throughout its life, first as a restaurant, then a hotel and lastly as a public house. The front elevation of the building collapsed in 1980 and the rest of the building was demolished.

TOP: **CHILDREN IN THE MOUTH OF A REPLICA WHALE, BELLE VUE, 1955**. Known as "Willie", the real whale was housed in an aquarium in the children's zoo.

ABOVE: **BELLE VUE, 1903**. Buffalo Bill and his wild west circus were regular visitors to Belle Vue. The show included portrayals of a buffalo hunt, an Indian attack and even Custer's last stand.

LEFT: **MARKET STREET,** *c* 1950. The Church of England Whit Sunday walk parades down Market Street. Whit Walks took place on Whitsuntide — the seventh Sunday after Easter — when children carrying posies and banners paraded from their local churches to the city centre. It was customary for children to wear a new set of clothes for the occasion. The walks were watched by thousands of people who gathered along the pavements in front of the shops, bringing the city centre to a standstill.

SPORT

Sport and leisure have always been a fundamental part of life in Manchester, the home of two famous top-class football teams as well as Lancashire Cricket Club. Athletes and supporters from all over the globe come to the city to participate in and enjoy sport

RIGHT: **OLD TRAFFORD, 1930.** Founded in 1892, for its first nine years Manchester United Football Club was called Newton Heath. The team shown here finished 22nd in league division 1 with 22 points.

BELOW: **FA CUP FINAL, WEMBLEY, 1934.** Sam Cowan, Manchester City captain, accepts the trophy after the team's victory over Portsmouth in 1934. Sam Cowan was appointed player-manager at Mossley in 1937. He died in 1964 aged 62 after collapsing whilst refereeing a charity cricket match in aid of wicket-keeper Jim Parks.

ABOVE: **MAINE ROAD, 1950.** Bert Trautmann, City's famous German goalkeeper, is swamped by autograph-hunters outside the Maine Road ground. Trautmann spent part of the war at a POW camp in Ashton and was brought to the club in 1949 by manager John Thomson — a highly controversial move which sparked a demonstration of 40,000 people on the city streets. Trautmann eventually won the hearts and minds of the Maine Road fans and was awarded the OBE in 2004.

ABOVE: **OLD TRAFFORD, 1959.** United moved from their old ground at Bank Street, Clayton to a brand-new stadium at Old Trafford. For its day, Old Trafford was a state of the art facility with terracing on three sides and a covered main stand with seating. It was designed by the famous Scottish architect Archibald Leitch, who built many other football stadiums including Hampden Park. Old Trafford was badly bomb-damaged during the Second World War and United played their home games at Maine Road from 1946-49.

RIGHT: OLD TRAFFORD CRICKET GROUND, 1957. The Warwick Road ground hosted a three-day match that summer between Lancashire and the West Indies. The Windies won by nine wickets.

INSET: LANCASHIRE WOMAN CRICKETER, 1938. The history of women's cricket stretches back at least 250 years: the first recorded match in England was between Bramley and Hambleton in 1745. The first county match was in 1931 between Durham and a combined Lancashire and Cheshire side.

RIGHT: OLD TRAFFORD, 1910. Lancashire Cricket Club team members pose for a photograph. This was a memorable season which saw some exciting matches with Lancashire finishing fourth in the league. By a remarkable coincidence, two sets of brothers (both by the name of Tyldesley) played first-class cricket for the county in this year.

LEFT: OLD TRAFFORD, MAY 4 1938. Warwick Road has been the home of Lancashire County Cricket Club since 1856 and international matches have been played there since 1884. In this, the first match of the season, two players walk out to the crease in a match between Lancashire and Worcestershire. Lancashire won by 10 wickets.

ABOVE: ROCHDALE HORNETS, 1950. Formed in 1871, Rochdale Hornets were founder members of the Rugby League. The club was at its strongest in the first two decades of the 20th century and won the Challenge Cup in the 1921-22 season. For most of their history until 1988, Hornets played at the famous Rochdale Athletics Ground.

ABOVE: ROCHDALE HORNETS GRANDSTAND CRASH, 1939. Tragedy struck at the Athletics Ground on April 1 when the main stand collapsed. Two spectators were killed and 15 others taken to hospital. The ground was packed when the roof of the stand gave way under the weight of spectators climbing onto the roof to get a better view.

THE CITY AT WAR

Manchester played a major role in both world wars and supplied large numbers of troops and armaments. As a centre of heavy industry, the city suffered badly from bombing during the Second World War. In true tradition, Manchester people rallied round to protect the vulnerable and to help defeat the enemy

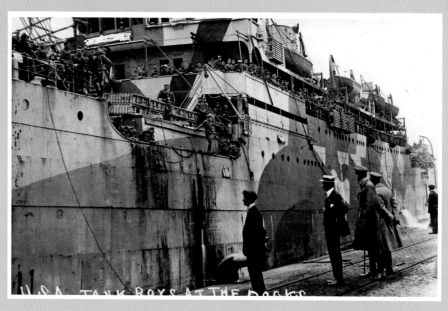

ABOVE: **ALBERT SQUARE, 1915.** Lord Kitchener visits Manchester. Kitchener had completely re-organised the army into 69 divisions by April 1915, 30 of which were made up of volunteers, many from Manchester and Liverpool.

ABOVE: **USA TANK BOYS, SALFORD DOCKS, 1914.** Although American forces did not enter the First World War until April 1917, the US regularly sent boats with equipment and specialist help to the Allies throughout the early years of the war.

ABOVE: **COLLYHURST, 1940.** In true *Dad's Army* fashion, a proud Home Guard battalion marches through Collyhurst. These volunteers had been promised uniforms and arms but as can be seen here their uniform consisted of little more than a roughly made arm band and their weapons amounted to a collection of pitchforks, broomsticks and makeshift rifles.
LEFT: **EVACUATION, 1939.** During September 1939, 72,000 children and 32,000 adults were voluntarily evacuated from the city. Some went as far afield as the Lake District but many only moved to the edge of the city to avoid the worst of the bombing. Towards the end of the war, when bombing was at its most intense in the south of the country, many children were moved from London to Manchester.

ABOVE: **WARTIME PICCADILLY, 1940.** During the war, the gardens were transformed into giant bomb shelters. Despite civil defences such as these, there was heavy loss of life in the Manchester Blitz. Information about civilian casualties and damage to areas such as Trafford Park was kept out of the news by order of the government so as not to spread despondency and alarm among the city's population.

THE MANCHESTER BLITZ, TOP, ABOVE AND LEFT. Between July 1940 and June 1941, Manchester suffered a number of devastating air raids. The raids on the nights of December 22 and 23 were particularly bad killing over 700 people and badly damaging Manchester Cathedral, Old Trafford football ground and the Royal Exchange. The Free Trade Hall (top) was left in ruins. Manchester had been hit by one of the heaviest incendiary attacks of the war and a firestorm quickly engulfed much of the city centre. Spectators reported seeing the flames from the moors 20 miles away. Winston Churchill (above) visits the devastated scene at the Free Trade Hall and St Peter's Street after the December raids. The prime minister surveys the ruins as he stands with local dignitaries amidst the carnage. The Free Trade Hall was so extensively damaged that it was not re-opened until 1951.

IN AND AROUND MANCHESTER

Originally a collection of separate towns and villages, the many districts around the city gradually merged into one urban area. Each district retained its own distinctive character: the areas to the north of the centre reflect much of the city's industrial past, while the leafy southern side, which was originally home to the wealthy cotton barons and industrialists, soon became the fashionable place to live for Manchester's middle-class professionals

RIGHT: **SALFORD CENTRAL LIBRARY AND ART GALLERY, 1958.** The *Then and Now* exhibition is in full swing as beautifully dressed girls in 1950s frocks make their way towards the entrance. Built in the 1850s the gallery forms the centrepiece of a set of buildings. It houses a fine collection of Victorian art and sculpture; the paintings of LS Lowry were displayed in the gallery before Salford's new Lowry centre was built.

LEFT AND BELOW: **DRINKING FOUNTAIN, 1890 & CHEETHAM HILL VILLAGE, 1905.** In Victorian times Cheetham was one of Manchester's most desirable areas. The historic home of Manchester's Jewish community, in recent decades it has become somewhat rundown but is now the focus of a major regeneration programme which will see the transformation of the area.

ABOVE: **ANCOATS, 1900.** Civic dignitaries at the laying of a foundation stone at the Pipe Stores off Oldham Road. Just a short walk from the city centre, Ancoats was the world's first industrial suburb. In the mid 19th century it was packed with back-to-back houses for the workers who laboured in the area's textile mills. Many of the surviving mills are now listed and Ancoats today is a conservation area.

RIGHT, BELOW AND FAR RIGHT:
THREE VIEWS OF CRUMPSALL.
The first, an aerial view from 1925 is of Crumpsall, Manchester and Prestwich Hospital; the British Dyestuffs Corporation and Crumpsall Vale are in the background. The hospital was built between 1866-70 and was designed by the architect Thomas Worthington (1826-1909). Originally the Prestwich Union workhouse, the buildings are now part of the North Manchester General Hospital. The second, a postcard from 1924, is of the Church of St Matthew with St Mary, Cleveland Road. The third dates from 1907 and shows pupils and staff at Crumpsall Lane Municipal School.

ST. MATTHEW'S CHURCH, CRUMPSALL.

LEFT: **HARPURHEY, 1934.** Postmen pass the time of day at the junction of Rochdale Road and Queens Road. Like neighbouring Crumpsall, Moston and Blackley, Harpurhey became a centre for dyeing and bleaching. Andrews Dyeworks came to dominate the town's commercial affairs. Harpurhey Cemetery, later to become the Manchester General Cemetery, was opened in 1868 with landscaped gardens and a catacomb. The country village of Harpurhey was soon swallowed up by industrialisation in the late 19th century and was incorporated into Manchester in 1885.

LEFT AND ABOVE: TWO VIEWS OF BLACKLEY: CRAB LANE 1908 AND BOOTH HALL CHILDREN'S HOSPITAL *c* 1959. The Booth Hall Infirmary was built in 1907 using the rubble from the house of local philanthropist Humphrey Booth. In 1914 the hospital developed a children's unit which rapidly became one of the leading children's hospitals in the country.

LEFT: MOSTON BOTTOMS, 1934. The Irk Valley region was a flourishing mining community and contained many properties like these small cottages in the Bottoms. This was the original home of the Moston Brook animal sanctuary — an 'informal' sanctuary that was a feature of the locality in the 1950s.

RIGHT: COLLYHURST, 1909. A cottage in Hendham Vale, part of the Irk Valley, which was demolished in 1917. The Queen's Road railway viaduct is in the distance. Collyhurst had once been a leafy suburb but the discovery of coal in the mid 19th century led to its rapid expansion with many houses being built for the workers at St George's Colliery. By the end of the century Collyhurst was heavily industrialised and very polluted with a dye works, papermill, rope works and brickworks all belching fumes into the atmosphere.

RIGHT: **CLAYTON, 1928.** A tram glides along the cobbled surface of Ashton New Road as people cross near the handsome Conservative club. The Industrial Revolution propelled Clayton from its earlier status as a small village into a hive of industry. Its position close to the Ashton Canal meant that it was an important link in the transport network but it was also the site of a chemical works, which led to pollution in the nearby River Medlock. While decline and dereliction followed after the war, Clayton is now benefiting from the influx of funds associated with the development of the City of Manchester Stadium (the site of the 2002 Commonwealth Games).

RIGHT: **MILES PLATTING,** *c* 1936. A view of the Oldham Road and Queens Road area. For much of the 19th and early 20th centuries Miles Platting was an area of densely-packed workers' housing, textile mills, a tannery, gasworks and a chemical works carved through by railway lines and sidings. Buildings were covered in soot and grime and the area was heavily polluted.

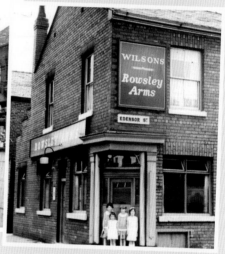

ABOVE AND LEFT: views of **BESWICK** and neighbouring **OPENSHAW**, both taken in 1963, that could have come straight from *Coronation Street*. The children above are in the doorway of the Rowsley Arms on the corner of Edenson Street while those on the left are standing on the corner of Bowness Street.

In post-war years the streetscape of Beswick and Openshaw changed fundamentally as the Victorian terraces were swept away in slum clearance programmes.

For most of the last two centuries heavy industry dominated the area with two massive concerns located nearby — the Armstrong Whitworth Ordnance Factory and the Beyer Peacock locomotive yards. These two enterprises sucked in workers and the population expanded dramatically in the 19th century. The decline of heavy industry in the 20th century saw the population fall to a fraction of its previous figure; now the people of Openshaw and Beswick are benefiting from regeneration and looking forward to the arrival of new businesses in the area.

LEFT AND BELOW: **TWO VIEWS OF ARDWICK.** The busy Stockport Road, seen below in 1934, runs through Ardwick into the city centre. By the late 19th century the pleasant suburb had been absorbed into the grimy heart of Manchester and had its share of mills and other kinds of "works" along the River Medlock. Between 1879-1880 a school for the education of poor boys was built on Hyde Road, Ardwick. Called the Nicholls Hospital, its architect was Thomas Worthington — the runner-up in the competition to build Manchester Town Hall. It was financed from a bequest by Benjamin Nicholls, the son of a local mill-owning family who died at the age of 36. During the Second World War it was used as a barracks for troops, the pupils having been transferred to Chethams School. In 1953 it was purchased by the local education authority and re-opened as the Nicholls County Secondary School for Boys. In 2002 the building was magnificently restored and is now the Manchester College for Arts and Technology.

LEFT: **STOCKPORT ROAD, LONGSIGHT 1958.** Longsight's earliest development owes much to its position on the ancient road between Buxton and Manchester. At the junction of Slade Lane and the Stockport Road there was a toll booth around which other buildings soon gathered. In the 1830s, the establishment and expansion of Belle Vue Gardens fuelled development which was also helped by the location of railway maintenance yards in the area.

ABOVE: **IN SEARCH OF A STORY.** By 1960, the Longsight Free Christian church in Birch Lane was being used by the BBC.

ABOVE: **SUNNYBROW PARK, GORTON,** *c* **1906.** Adults and children enjoy the pleasures of Sunnybrow Park. In the distance is Brookfield Unitarian Church. It was built in 1870 and endowed by Richard Peacock, an engineer who became Gorton's first MP.

ABOVE: **TAN YARD BROW, GORTON, 1904.** A tannery operated in this area until 1958 giving this hill its distinctive name. The green spaces of Debdale Park off the Hyde Road provided locals with welcome relief from the bustle of the local streets and factories.

ABOVE: a rush cart outside the **PLOUGH HOTEL, GORTON,** *c* **1910.** In the week before the annual rush-bearing ceremony in the local churches, a cart was taken round each of the local hotels and pubs in turn. On the day itself, fresh rushes were laid in each church and the old rushes burnt along with the cart.

ABOVE: **LEAF STREET BATHS, HULME, 1920.** This splendid establishment was built in 1860 by the architect Thomas Worthington. Along with Turkish baths and more conventional "single" baths, Leaf Street also boasted a laundry and state of the art spin-dryers. These facilities were vitally important for the residents of Hulme: the once leafy village saw its population grow from 1,677 in 1801 to more than 150,000 by the mid 19th century. Most people lived in appalling conditions — one contemporary report speaks of up to 300 people sharing one lavatory.

RIGHT: **GROCER'S SHOP HULME, 1939.** In the days before superstores corner shops like this one flourished, providing everything from cooked meat and cheese, to yeast and snuff.

LEFT: **TRAFFORD PARK,** *c* **1910.** By the early years of the 20th century the Ship Canal was helping to bring new prosperity to Manchester. Within 10 years of its opening more than 40 companies had moved to the newly established Trafford Park industrial estate, establishing this as the world's first industrial park. By 1945 over 75,000 people worked there. The triumphal arch, pictured here, was erected for a trade exhibition.

RIGHT: **LEVENSHULME, 1907.** Levenshulme is situated on the Manchester to Stockport Road. In the centre of the picture is the Levenshulme Town Hall. The council offices were moved in 1950 when the town was incorporated into the city of Manchester; the town hall is now the Levenshulme Antiques Village. The two sets of tramlines carried passengers from Manchester to Bullock Smithy.

LEFT: **WILMSLOW ROAD, FALLOWFIELD, c 1910.** A tram on its way into the city centre passes elegantly dressed ladies seated on Wilmslow Road. This tram called at Lapwing Lane terminus before reaching Rusholme.

ABOVE: **FIRE STATION, MOSS SIDE, 1906.** The Moss Side Fire Brigade proudly display their fire engine outside the new fire station. Built in the Alexandra Park area, the fire station and equipment was an example of the facilities that new wealth was bringing to the city.

LEFT: **NEW SCHOOL, MOSS SIDE, 1893.** Crowds gather around the site of the Princess Road Board School to watch the ceremony of the laying of the foundation stone. The size of the gathering shows the importance of the occasion for the local community.

ABOVE: **CHORLTON GREEN, 1928**. Even today, Chorlton-cum-Hardy retains the feel of a country village. A group gather in front of the Horse and Jockey public house overlooking the picturesque Green. Although the original building dates from 1550 the pub only acquired its half-timbered façade around 1910.

TOP RIGHT: **ZETLAND ROAD, CHORLTON, 1959**. The corner of Zetland Road, Sandy Lane and Barlow Moor Road appears an almost idyllic backwater with few vehicles in this late fifties photograph. The handsome Zetland Terrace built in 1883 dominates the view.

RIGHT: **HORSE-DRAWN DELIVERY VAN, CHORLTON, 1949**. A Manchester and District Co-op bakery horse van stands on St Clements Road.

ABOVE: **WITHINGTON**, *c* 1910. A view towards Withington village from the junction of Parsonage Road. The library is in the distance.

ABOVE RIGHT: **WITHINGTON**, *c* 1950. The same view 40 years later, this time looking down the road from the library, shows an increase in private cars and an absence of tramlines.

LEFT: **BURNAGE**, *c* 1910. Burnage was once described by George Bernard Shaw as the prettiest village in Manchester. The area developed a cottage industry in handweaving and many of the original weaver's cottages still exist in Burnage Lane. In 1910, Burnage Garden Village — a garden suburb — was built with many new semi-detached houses and recreational facilities including a village hall, allotments, tennis courts and a children's playground. The garden village was completed in 1912 and soon became a fashionable suburb for professional people and their families.

LEFT: **DIDSBURY**, *c* 1935. The Didsbury Hotel and Ye Olde Cock Inn built in 1909 stand either side of the entrance to Fletcher Moss House and Gardens, home of the former Alderman Fletcher Moss. The gateway was bought for £10 when the Spread Eagle Hotel was demolished.

BELOW: **GALLEON POOL, DIDSBURY, 1953.** Adults and children enjoy the outdoor Galleon Pool in Didsbury, not far from Parrs Wood junction. The area has now been developed as an hotel and leisure club.

ABOVE: **PUBLIC GARDENS DIDSBURY, 1957.** Fletcher Moss Gardens were given to the city in 1914 by Alderman Fletcher Moss, a keen botanist, who lived in the nearby parsonage. The 10-acre park and gardens became famous for their botanical displays, orchid house and exotic plants.

LEFT: **RUSHOLME**, *c* 1922. This photograph is taken standing on Wilmslow Road, looking towards Dickenson Road with Platt Fields in the distance. The Birch Vale Hotel on the left-hand side attracted many local customers. It was in the Congregational church built on Wilmslow Road in 1864 that Herbert Asquith, later to become prime minister, married Helen Melland in 1867.

LEFT: **WYTHENSHAWE HALL,** *c* **1920.** This Tudor half-timbered house was the home of the Tatton family for over 400 years. Built around 1540, the family sold most of the surrounding land for housing development to Manchester City Council in 1926. The hall is still open for visitors today.

BELOW LEFT: **FISHMONGERS, NORTHENDEN, 1959.** On the corner of Brett Street, formerly Brown Street on Palatine Road, stands the famous seafood shop Mac Fisheries. Many older residents remember the tiled floors and marble counters.

BELOW: **CINEMA, NORTHENDEN, 1959.** The ABC or Forum Cinema opened in 1934. It contained a Wurlitzer organ and put on many stage shows. This Art Deco building has found a new use today as a meeting place for Jehovah's Witnesses.

Acknowledgment

Thanks to Sara, my eldest daughter, for all her help and support with the book.

Dedication

I have always had support and love from my mum and dad. I could not have done all that I have to date without their help. You will be with me always now and forever.

First published in 2005 by Myriad Books Limited
35 Bishopsthorpe Road London SE26 4PA

Photographs © Manchester City Library Archives and Local Studies Unit

Text © Robert Gibb
www.gibbsbookshop.co.uk

ISBN 1 904 736 87 4

Designed by Jerry Goldie Graphic Design

Printed in China

www.myriadbooks.com